Wisdom with Understanding is Better Than Rubies

Lurine Karon Greenberg
Fine Arts Collection

Cafés & Restaurants

Edited by / Herausgegeben von:
Laura Andreini
Nicola Flora
Paolo Giardiello
Gennaro Postiglione

 teNeues

Editor in chief
Marco Casamonti

Editorial coordination
Davide Musmeci

Editor
Federica Passoni

Graphic design
Studio tre

Original book title: caffé e ristoranti

English translation: John M. King
German translation: Britta Nord
Production: Werkstatt München · Martin Waller

Published in US and Canada by teNeues Publishing Company

Published in Germany by teNeues Verlag GmbH + Co. KG

Published in UK and Ireland by teNeues Publishing UK Ltd.

www.teneues.com

Die Deutsche Bibliothek – CIP-Einheitsaufnahme
Ein Titeldatensatz für diese Publikation ist bei der Deutschen Bibliothek erhältlich.

ISBN 3-8238-5478-X
Printed in Italy

contents
inhalt

Spaces offering hospitality:
cafés, bars, restaurants, pubs

Coming to grips with the architecture of a city, grasping
the extent to which architectonic creations match the
exigencies and the cultural growth of a society means
shunning places representing officialdom – public buildings, museums, administration centres and the like.
One has to descend to realms closer to daily life and
their changing, contradictory aspects; one has to enter
homes, to buy things in shops, to seek refreshment in
a small bar. It is in these places that one discovers the
parts of the city where people go about their daily
existence, sites of sudden change and developments in
the quest for the latest fashion, craze or taste; these bul-
warks of tradition and forged habits are part and parcel
of the city "way of life". Compared to private spheres, to
the intimate, specific nature of domestic living space,
especially these public places represent an interesting
"half-way house" in architec-tural planning; on the one
hand, they involve the typical problems of planning interiors more closely related to man's physical and psychological requirements; on the other hand, they are con-
ditioned by having to serve a large number of people,
whose imaginary nature assumes, at times unconscious-
ly, the real character of the establishment.
Spaces that doubtless influence and form the character
of a city are these establishments offering refreshment
and the chance to meet friends: the little bars where one
stops to read a book or a newspaper, to have a chat,
where one drops by for a quick *espresso* – with one eye
on the clock inexorably striking the beat of everyday
life – or where one sips one's tea in pleasant company,
oblivious to the passage of time. The bars, the cafés, the
fast food restaurants, the *trattorie* or the more elegant
restaurants that invite us to indulge in fine delicacies
have become the stage for today's social life. Now they
have intentionally discarded the image previously fos-
tered by country inns and local pubs and clubs – places
of the past, formerly loyal custodians and testimonies
of everyday traditions and rites; today's bars, pubs and

4

restaurants are stepping up their efforts to tune into the needs of different typologies of users.

To say that they are followers of fashion is perhaps a rather one-sided view, for they often precede fashion or even create it; the truth is that they have become social phenomena in constant flux, seeking to portray or reflect society in their own right. Of all public places they are perhaps the most transitory, exhibiting a frenetic propensity towards renewal, constantly in the public eye due to their inherent indispensability.

The planning of such establishments has thus been the subject of considerable research and experimentation, not only by architects but also by designers, artists, innovators from the world of fashion often proposing new materials and solutions intended to cater for a critical public. In fact, they have continually created synergies between the fields of architecture, furnishing, decor, visual arts and graphic art, incorporating music, advertising and multimedia.

It is this "experimental", irreverent character that distinguishes it from the architecture of buildings and largescale urban schemes. On the one hand, the planning of such settings often pursues strategies diverging from standard architectural research; on the other hand, expressive opportunities and potentialities of spaces are tested here in what may be termed *in vitro* experiments and later applied to buildings of different dimensions and purposes.

Materials that are less customary in building and tectonics, iridescent leathers, plasma screens transmitting life-size images intermingle with precious woods, polished marble, bricks and metals with a flair of antiquity. Examples such as the large-scale transformations of Barcelona or Berlin, now seen from a distance in time, point to a phase when the planning of the interiors of the bars and restaurants is disassociating itself, sometimes controversially, from the architecture of stone and technology, generally opting for another of more external influences, of blurred contours, where one field of activity and research influences and stimulates the other. The collection of achievements, highly varied and het-

erogeneous, presented in this publication can be inter-
preted either as a cross-section of a social phenomenon
in itself, autonomous and pertinent to a specific practice, or as a parallel, contemporaneous adventure – in a
juxtaposition of dates and places – through the history
of a generally known architecture. Both aspects are
directly related to the initial reasons and the final out-
come that characterise these works, where man with all
his contradictions takes the stage.

Differentiating between the various aspects in architectural planning, insisting on disciplinary autonomies
would not be correct, as it would probably trigger a
never-ending process of abstraction, neglecting the
complexities of social phenomena naturally addressed
by architecture as a whole and supplying it with its
prime stimuli. Specific disciplinary features do in fact
exist; they must be defended according to their significance.

Establishments providing refreshment fulfil several fun-
damental principles, the most important being that of
extending their guests a warm welcome. Within a public space they seek to offer the opportunities, qualities
and intensities of "being together" that are in fact in-

herent in the relationship formed in a private environ-
ment, when one invites guests to share one's own home.
The term "welcome" undoubtedly implies the idea of
"taking care" of one's guests, of dedicating oneself
to the reception of others in one's own living space, of
giving the new arrivals the feeling of being at home.
This act of welcoming is a moment of magic, the guest
feels he is the protagonist of a pleasant, carefully ar-
ranged event. Even in the setting of the home this prin-
ciple is not always easy to put into practice: the reception or welcome does not solely hinge on physical
factors relating to the order of the space.

A perfectly organised home, for example, may create an
impersonal atmosphere, in which the people living there
cannot be related to. This serious deficiency, despite
the existence of appropriate furniture and furnishings,
creates an air of incompleteness, even unfriendliness
without any signs of the everyday life taking place there.

Welcoming guests is a psychological condition in the person inviting them into the intimacy of his or her home, a place that is not only physical, as sharing these spheres implies the awareness of being together. The character of the host or hostess is revealed not via the objects in the ambience but through the image of him- or herself projected into these objects.

The welcome is thus a feature related to man's "presence", highlighting an essential requirement of the interior: the planning of the interiors by man must include man. Conceiving architecture from the interior means conceiving it through the eyes of the future beneficiary. The planning criteria must incorporate architecture and man as a whole, bearing in mind that neither can be restricted to reproducible, measurable canons and codes and that in particular the plan is only the beginning of a process in which the planner will be the first to leave and that will continue without his supervision or control.

The welcome is a category of behaviour found in public places where actions and relationships reproduce the intimacy typical of the private sphere. Having dinner, for example, meeting over a quick plate of pasta, or imbibing drinks evoke rituals derived from primordial activities such as eating and coming together. In public life these activities permit breaks in the flow of everyday life of work and human relations, in the form of little rites which, albeit increasingly performed in specific environments like these bars and restaurants, date back to older traditions of informal, family gestures and patterns of behaviour. The difference lies in the fact that these places are not the home of someone welcoming us but constitute a setting already characterised by acts of hospitality and contact with others. Whereas the home has to transfer its character from its structures and fittings to its occupants, environments such as bars or restaurants are compelled to focus on creating the necessary intimacy and atmosphere for its users. Places serving food and drink tend to construct hospitality, as it were, to provide a suitable setting for forging relationships, to inspire the necessary welcome. They provide a respite from public life, acting as collective spaces for activities otherwise reserved for the private sphere. The enormous variety in their taste and style thus seems perfectly justified, as they have to fulfil to the best of their ability criteria of a personal, inscrutable nature. Addressing one type of user rather than another creates the image – sometimes more austere and decadent, sometimes unconventional and temporary – which they seek to suggest via their conformity, materials, fittings and embellishments.

These places, as presented in this book in their ensemble, represent a cross-section of the society of recent years: some are born of tastes already formed, others suggest using space in the way we normally find in the home; some seem to date further back, others still have to find their place in the history of habitation. But they all clearly reflect the lives of the people frequenting them, who have decreed their success or failure according to their virtues or weaknesses, who have positioned them in the spaces of urban life as oases and sanctuaries, as small monuments of everyday life.

A. F. G. P.

Orte der Gastlichkeit:
Cafés, Bars, Restaurants, Kneipen

Um die Architektur einer Stadt wirklich zu verstehen, um zu begreifen, wie sehr die Bauwerke die Bedürfnisse und die kulturelle Entwicklung einer Gesellschaft widerspiegeln, darf man nicht danach gehen, wie sie sich offiziell präsentiert – wie öffentliche Bauten, Museen, Amtsgebäude aussehen –, sondern muss sich an den wechselhaften und widersprüchlichen Facetten der Räume orientieren, die stärker vom menschlichen Alltag durchdrungen sind: Wohnhäuser, Geschäfte, kleine Cafés. Denn dies sind die Teile der Stadt, in denen die Menschen tatsächlich ihr Leben verbringen, Räume, die entweder sehr stark der Mode und dem Zeitgeschmack unterliegen oder aber als Bollwerk der Tradition und Ort jener eingefleischten Gewohnheiten fungieren, die den „Lebensstil" einer Stadt ausmachen. Vor allem den Lokalen kommt dabei eine interessante Zwitterstellung in der Architektur zu. Wie private Räume müssen sie den seelischen und physischen Bedürfnissen eines nach innen gekehrten, individuellen häuslichen Wohnens Rechnung tragen, andererseits sind sie für eine große Anzahl von Menschen bestimmt und müssen von daher gänzlich andere Erwartungen erfüllen. Lokale sind Gebäude, die den Charakter einer Stadt besonders deutlich erkennen lassen – und ihn in erheblichem Maße mitbestimmen. Es sind Orte, die man aufsucht, um in Ruhe die Zeitung oder ein Buch zu lesen, an denen man sich aber auch mit Freunden trifft; Orte, an denen man mit einem besorgten Blick auf die Zeiger der Uhr, die den unerbittlichen Rhythmus des Arbeitstages vorgeben, schnell etwas zu sich nimmt – oder wo man in geselliger Runde einen ganzen Abend verbringen kann. In Bars, Cafés, Imbisslokalen, einfachen Gaststätten oder Restaurants mit exquisitem Speisenangebot spielen sich immer größere Teile des gesellschaftlichen Lebens ab. Bars, Cafés und Restaurants grenzen sich dabei heute bewusst von ländlichen Wirtshäusern oder den Kneipen an der Ecke mit ihrem Image als Horte der Erinnerung, der Tradition und der Gewohnheit ab und passen sich, wie bequeme und praktische Kleidungsstücke, immer mehr den wechselnden Bedürfnissen verschiedener Gruppen von Nutzern an.

Zu behaupten, dass diese Lokale mit der Mode gehen, ist eher zu wenig gesagt; oft sind sie ihrer Zeit voraus, prägen einen Stil, übernehmen Vorbildfunktion – sie sind kulturelle Phänomene, die sich beständig weiterentwickeln und dem Drang der Gesellschaft, sich selbst darzustellen, auf vielfältige, wenn auch kurzlebige Weise Ausdruck verleihen. Von allen öffentlichen Räumen sind sie sicherlich diejenigen, die den stärksten Veränderungen unterworfen sind, die ihre Ausstattung in verblüffendem Tempo wechseln, und doch sind sie als Institution so wichtig, ja unentbehrlich, dass das Interesse des Publikums an ihnen nie nachlässt.

Mit der Planung dieser Räume sind daher nicht nur Architekten befasst, sondern auch Designer, Künstler und Modeschöpfer, die mit neuartigen Materialien und originellen Ideen die wachsenden Ansprüche einer selbstbewussten Kundschaft zu erfüllen suchen. Die Architektur verschmilzt zu einer Einheit mit der Einrichtung und der Dekoration, mit Elementen der bildenden Kunst und der Grafik, ja sogar mit Musik, Werbung und multimedialen Ausdrucksformen. Dieser bisweilen provozierend „experimentelle" Charakter ist es, was Lokale von anderen Gebäuden und städteplanerischen Großprojekten unterscheidet: Einerseits gehen die Entwürfe für solche Räume weit über die Planung rein baulicher Maßnahmen hinaus, andererseits werden in diesen Projekten immer häufiger Möglichkeiten der Raumgestaltung, sozusagen *in vitro*, erprobt, die später auch in Bauten anderer Größenordnung und Funktion verwirklicht werden. Für das Bauwesen ungewöhnliche Materialien wie schillerndes Leder oder Plasmabildschirme mit lebensgroßen Darstellungen werden nicht selten mit kostbaren Hölzern, schimmerndem Marmor, Ziegeln und patinierten Metallen kombiniert.

10

Wenn man tief greifende Veränderungen des Stadtbildes wie in Barcelona oder in Berlin aus einer gewissen zeitlichen Distanz heraus betrachtet, werden zwei jeweils aufeinander folgende Tendenzen sichtbar. Zunächst wird die Innengestaltung der Lokale teilweise demonstrativ von der gängigen, von Stein und Technologie beherrschten Architektur abgesetzt, anschließend findet eine gewisse Annäherung zwischen beiden Bereichen statt, die Grenzen verwischen sich, konventionelle und unkonventionelle Gestaltungsansätze beeinflussen und befruchten sich gegenseitig.

Die vorliegende Sammlung von höchst unterschiedlichen Projekten kann und soll auf zweierlei Weise interpretiert werden: zum einen als Querschnitt durch einen eigenständigen, aus ganz bestimmten Bedingungen heraus entstandenen Bereich des kulturellen Schaffens, zum anderen als Dokument einer Entwicklung, die – sowohl zeitlich als auch im Hinblick auf die Orte, an denen sie stattfindet – parallel zu der bekannteren und in vielen Veröffentlichungen gewürdigten Geschichte der Architektur verläuft. Beide Aspekte kommen bei der Planung und Realisierung dieser Werke zum Tragen; Lokale sind Bauten, bei denen in jeder Hinsicht der Mensch – mit all seinen Widersprüchen – die zentrale Rolle spielt. Spezielle Aspekte des gestalterischen Prozesses herauszugreifen, um die einzelnen Gattungen – Architektur, Einrichtung oder auch Dekoration – um jeden Preis isoliert zu betrachten, kann nicht Sinn der Sache sein. Eine solche Abstraktion verkäme zwangsläufig zum Selbstzweck und man liefe Gefahr, die Komplexität der gesellschaftlichen Zusammenhänge, auf die sich die Architektur als solche bezieht und aus denen sie sich speist, aus dem Blick zu verlieren. Dennoch bewahren sich die verschiedenen Disziplinen ihre spezifische Eigenständigkeit, allerdings in Abhängigkeit von den Möglichkeiten und Funktionen eines Projekts und den Absichten, die damit verfolgt werden.

Aus der Sicht ihrer Besucher erfüllen Lokale einige wichtige Funktionen des menschlichen Zusammenlebens, allen voran das Empfangen von Gästen. Man versucht, in einem Lokal – das heißt in einem öffentlichen Raum – jene Vielfalt, Qualität und Intensität zu erreichen, die auch das Beisammensein im privaten Bereich hat, wenn eine Person andere Personen zu sich einlädt und bei sich aufnimmt. Die Vorstellung vom „Empfangen" und „Aufnehmen" von Gästen beinhaltet eine gewisse Fürsorge gegenüber den fremden Personen, die sich im eigenen Raum aufhalten, das Bemühen darum, dass diese den Raum, in dem sie sich befinden, als ihren eigenen ansehen.

Das Empfangen eines Gastes ist eine beinahe schon magische Handlung: Der Gast wird in eine sorgfältig und eigens für ihn erschaffene Welt gezaubert, in der sich alles um ihn dreht. Das ist allerdings auch im häuslichen Rahmen nicht einfach zu verwirklichen, schließlich hängt die Gastlichkeit eines Hauses nicht nur von physischen Faktoren wie der Aufteilung eines Raums ab. Ein Haus kann noch so perfekt aufgebaut sein – Räume allein vermögen keine Beziehung zu ihren Nutzern herzustellen, dazu bedarf es eines Menschen, eben des Gastgebers.

11

Ein Haus kann, auch wenn es über die nötige Ausstattung und Einrichtung verfügt, unvollkommen, ja sogar abweisend erscheinen, wenn es nicht mit Leben erfüllt ist. Durch das Empfangen entsteht eine emotionale Beziehung zwischen dem Gast und demjenigen, der ihn in die Privatsphäre seiner Wohnung einlädt. Das Haus ist mehr als eine bloße Örtlichkeit; Voraussetzung für die gemeinsame Nutzung des Raums ist vielmehr das bewusste Zusammensein der beiden Personen. Wer oder was der Gastgeber ist, äußert sich nicht in den Dingen, die ihm gehören, sondern in dem Selbstbild, das diese Dinge reflektieren.

Das Empfangen von Gästen hat also mit der „Präsenz" des Menschen zu tun. Dies ist ein wesentlicher Aspekt des Innenraums. Die Planung von Innenräumen geht vom Menschen aus und muss diesen berücksichtigen. Ein Bauwerk von innen betrachten heißt, es aus dem Blickwinkel dessen zu sehen, der es nutzen wird. Für die Kriterien, die der Gestaltung zugrunde gelegt werden, heißt das, dass man Bau und Mensch als eine Einheit sehen muss, dass keiner von beiden sich in Raster abstrakter Kriterien pressen lässt und dass schließlich der Entwurf der Ausgangspunkt eines Prozesses ist, zu dem der Entwerfer lediglich den Anstoß geben kann, weil sich die weitere Entwicklung anschließend seiner Kontrolle entzieht.

Das Empfangen und Aufnehmen von Gästen wird dann zu einer Funktion des öffentlichen Raums, wenn dort persönliche Handlungen vollzogen und Beziehungen gepflegt werden, die normalerweise der Privatsphäre angehören. Zum Essen auszugehen oder sich irgendwo auf einen Happen oder ein Glas mit anderen zu treffen sind Rituale, die ursprünglich aus dem elementaren Bedürfnis nach Nahrungsaufnahme und zwischenmenschlichem Kontakt entstanden sind. Sie werden nun in der Öffentlichkeit ausgeübt und unterbrechen den alltäglichen Rhythmus aus Arbeit und zwischenmenschlichen Beziehungen mit kleinen ritualisierten Handlungen, die, auch wenn sie mit der Zeit in speziell auf diesen Zweck ausgerichtete Räume, wie eben Lokale, verlagert wurden, zum urtypischen familiären Verhalten des Menschen gehören. Der Unterschied besteht darin, dass diese Räume nicht das Heim eines Gastgebers sind, sondern nur die Bühne für Handlungen, die an sich schon Akte der Gastlichkeit und der Kontaktaufnahme mit anderen darstellen. Während in einer Wohnung die Bewohner und nicht die Aufteilung oder die Einrichtung der Räume die tragende Rolle spielen, ist es in Cafés und Restaurants Aufgabe der Raumgestaltung, eine Atmosphäre zu schaffen, in der sich die Besucher wohl fühlen. Lokale müssen also in gewisser Hinsicht Gastlichkeit erzeugen, müssen ein geeignetes Milieu für zwischenmenschliche Beziehungen bieten und Behaglichkeit verbreiten. Sie sind sozusagen „Zwischen-Räume" des öffentlichen Lebens, gemeinschaftliche Räume, in denen Menschen, auch im größeren Kreis, Handlungen vollziehen, die sonst auf die eigenen vier Wände beschränkt bleiben.

Dies erklärt auch, warum Lokale in ihrem Stil so unterschiedlich sind. Sie müssen ganz persönlichen – und deshalb kaum zu definierenden – Erwartungen so genau wie möglich entsprechen. Der Typus von Mensch, den man ansprechen will, bestimmt den Eindruck, den man durch die Raumgestaltung, die Materialien, die Einrichtung und die Dekoration zu vermitteln sucht – sei er eher nüchtern-ästhetisch oder mehr pfiffig-improvisiert. Alle diese Lokale zusammen bilden, wenn man wie in dem vorliegenden Band eines nach dem anderen betrachtet, einen repräsentativen Querschnitt der heutigen Gesellschaft: Manche sind in bewährtem Stil entstanden, andere lassen eine für Wohnräume typische Raumgestaltung erkennen, manche wirken etwas altmodisch, andere müssen sich ihren Platz in der Geschichte der Innenarchitektur wohl erst noch erobern. Und doch ist jedes Einzelne geprägt durch das Leben der Menschen, die dort ein- und ausgehen, die auf die eine oder andere Weise zu seinem Erfolg oder Misserfolg beigetragen haben und die es zu einer Oase, zu einem Zufluchtsort in der Stadtlandschaft gemacht haben, zu einem kleinen, aber wichtigen Denkmal des Alltags.

13

A.F.G.P.

Cafés & Restaurants

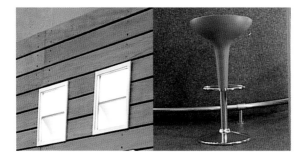

16

Sitio
1998

alfaro

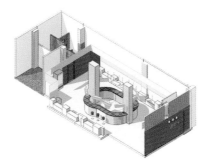

24

Stop Line
1995

archea

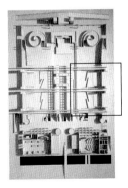

30

Euronet
1997

arribas

40

Gran Velvet
1993

arribas

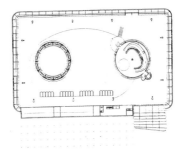

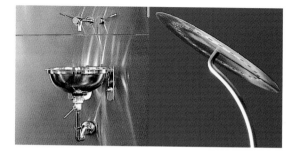

46

L'Arca
1997

boschi

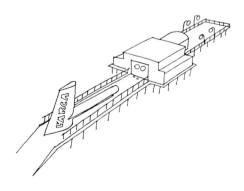

Women

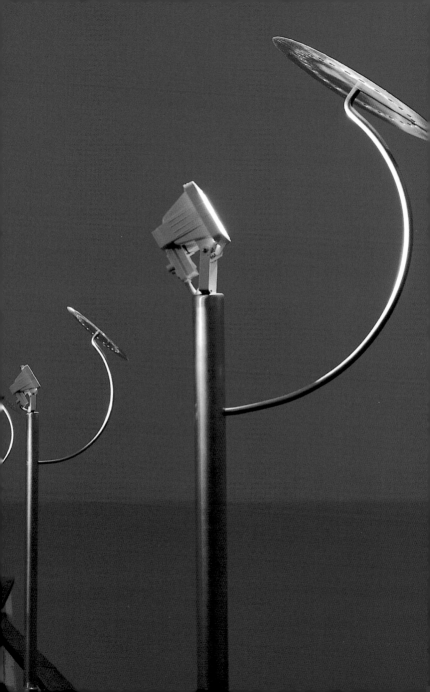

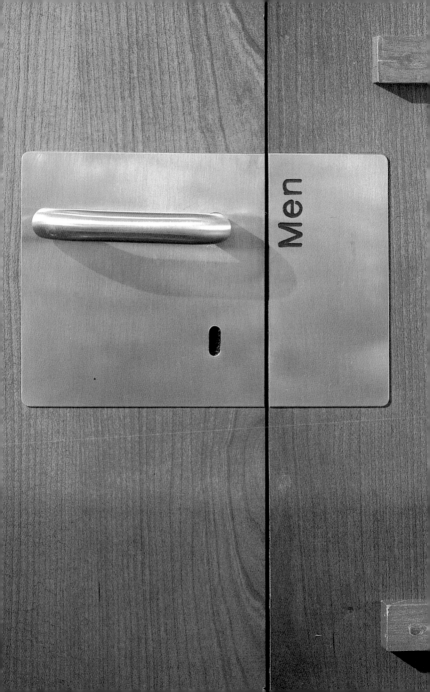

56

Bargo
1996

branson coates architecture

66

Giolitti Lunch & Tea
1991

cavaglià comoglio

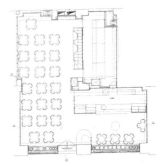

76

Orient-Express
1998

cavagnari

82

One Happy Cloud
1997

claesson koivisto rune architects

90

Servicio Wilson
1992

correa turull

100

Tragaluz
1990

cortes

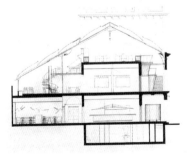

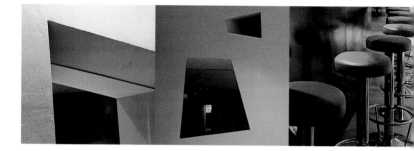

108

For Love or Money
1995

eusebi

118

Isola
1999

fin architects and designers inc.

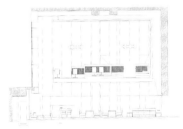

132

Reichstag
1999

foster and partners

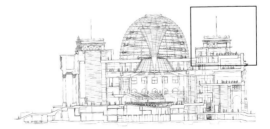

138

Dietrich's
1999

freixes varis arquitectes sl.

146

Nodo
1998

freixes varis arquitectes sl.

158

Zsa-Zsa Bar
1989

freixes miranda

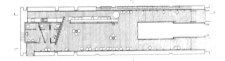

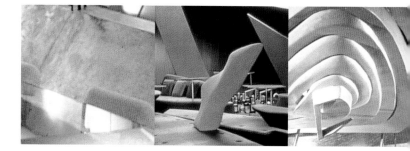

166

Moonsoon
1990

hadid

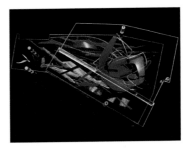

182

Georges
2000

jakob macfarlane

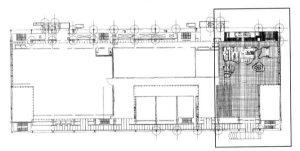

192

nil
1997

lazzarini pickering

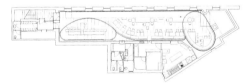

206

Blauw
1999

mecanoo architecten

216

Tubo
1993

miás pla salló

222

Peroni Music Cafè
1999

micheli

234

Blu Sonora
1999

monti muti

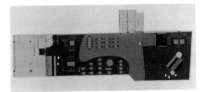

244

Tsunami
2000

morphosis

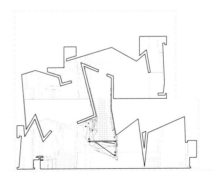

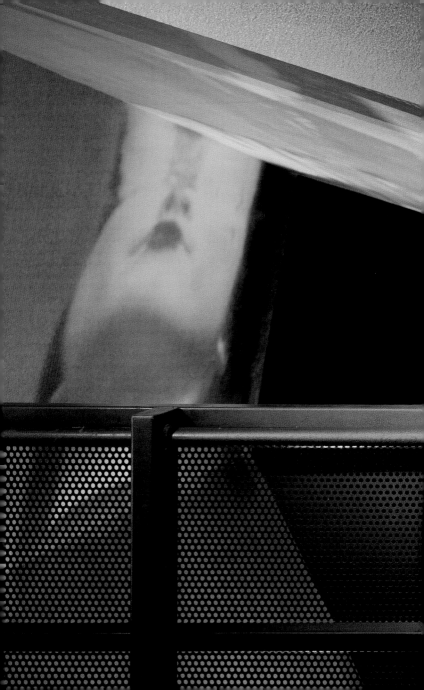

252

Universo
1993

nardi

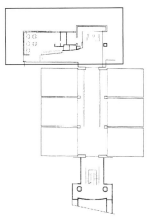

262

Schutzenberger
2000

nouvel

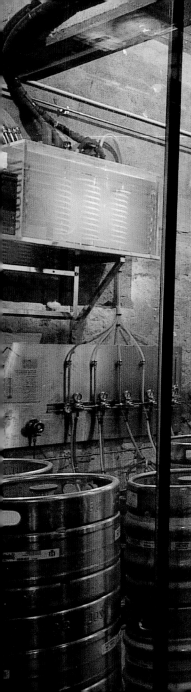

274

89
1995

ogawa depardon

282

El Racó
1999

pallí vert

288

Pharmacy
1998

rundell & associates ltd.

304

Epsylon
1989

santachiara

316

Hampton Club
1999

sapey

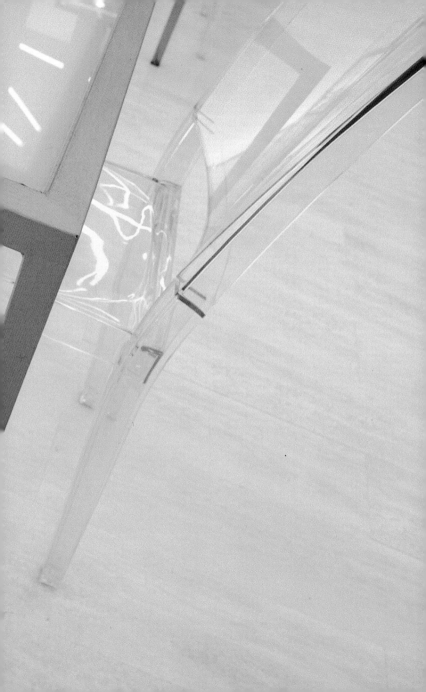

326

Bon
2000

starck

336

La Barraca
1995

uda volpe

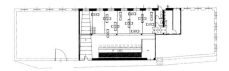

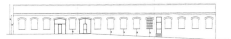

348

Bondst
1998

waisbrod studio gaia

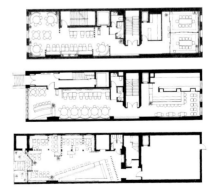

360

23 Michael Jordan
1999

waisbrod studio gaia

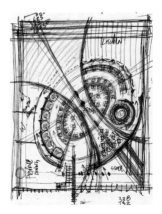

 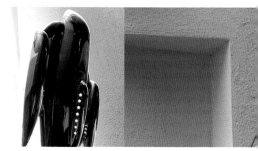

372

Nachtexpress
1990

windbichler

biographies

biografien

alfaro

Pedro José Javier Alfaro Bernal, born in Spain in 1953, graduates in architecture in Belgium and specialises as a decorator at the College of Applied Art in Pamplona. The founder and director of the international architecture journal "4'33", he produces during his twenty years of professional activity over 250 commercial works, mainly located in Pamplona, including the renovation of bars, hotels, factories and the creation of restaurants, shops and showrooms.

Pedro José Javier Alfaro Bernal wurde 1953 in Spanien geboren, studierte Architektur in Belgien und erwarb an der Schule für Angewandte Kunst in Pamplona eine Zusatzqualifikation als Raumausstatter. Er ist Begründer und Chefredakteur der internationalen Architekturzeitschrift „4'33" und hat in den 20 Jahren seiner beruflichen Tätigkeit mehr als 250 zum größten Teil in Pamplona gelegene gewerbliche Objekte realisiert. Dazu zählen die Renovierung von Bars, Hotels und Fabrikgebäuden sowie neu errichtete Restaurants, Geschäfte und Showrooms.

Project on page 17/
Projekt Seite 17
Bar Sitio
Pamplona, Spain/Spanien, 1998
Collaborators/Mitarbeit:
Ainhoa Sanz, Susana Martinez, Eva Lamana, Arantza Larrion, Marta Solano, Iñigo Lopez, Cristina Idoate
Photographer/Foto:
Alfonso Perkaz

archea

The Studio Archea Associati was founded in 1988 by Laura Andreini, Marco Casamonti and Giovanni Polazzi. The studio realises small- and large-scale works, ranging from interiors to architecture and urban schemes: the building of the "Centro Divertimenti di Curno", the Curno leisure centre, was selected and exhibited at the VI International Fair of Architecture of the Venice Biennale. Laura Andreini is an academic researcher in the field of architectural planning in Florence; Marco Casamonti is associate professor in Genoa and professor (under contract) of architectural planning in Florence. Since 1996 Giovanni Polazzi has been professor (under contract) of furnishings and interior architecture in Genoa and of planning in Florence. Marco Casamonti has been in charge of the international architecture magazine "Area" since 1995, where he is joined by Laura Andreini and Giovanni Polazzi. In 1998 the studio wins the planning competition for the new administrative and commercial centre at Calenzano and comes third in the competition for the new IUAV headquarters on the Magazzini Frigoriferi premises in San Basilio, Venice. Recent projects: the municipal library and auditorium (Curno, Bergamo, 1997); the services centre in San Maurizio d'Opaglio (Novara, 1999).

Das Studio Archea Associati wurde 1988 von Laura Andreini, Marco Casamonti und Giovanni Polazzi gegründet. Von den verschiedenen kleineren und größeren Projekten dieses Büros – Innenausstattungen, Bauten, urbane Projekte – wurde das Gebäude des Freizeitzentrums (Centro Divertimenti) in Curno ausgewählt und auf der VI. Internationalen Architekturausstellung der Biennale in Venedig gezeigt. Zusätzlich sind die drei Büroinhaber in Forschung und Lehre tätig. Laura Andreini hat eine Forschungsstelle im Fachbereich Bauprojektplanung in Florenz inne. Marco Casamonti ist Hochschuldozent in Genua und Professor (auf Zeit) für Bauprojektplanung in Florenz. Giovanni Polazzi ist seit 1996 Professor (auf Zeit) für Innenarchitektur in Genua, außerdem Professor für Bauprojektplanung in Florenz. Marco Casamonti leitet seit 1995 die internationale Architekturzeitschrift „Area", zu deren Mitarbeitern auch Laura Andreini und Giovanni Polazzi zählen. 1998 gewann das Büro den Wettbewerb für das neue Verwaltungs- und Handelszentrum in Calenzano und belegte den dritten Platz im Wettbewerb für den neuen Sitz des Istituto Universitario di Architettura di Venezia (IUAV) auf dem Gelände der Magazzini Frigoriferi in San Basilio, Venedig. Weitere Projekte jüngeren Datums sind die Gemeindebibliothek in Curno, Bergamo, zu der auch ein Veranstaltungssaal gehört (1997) sowie das Dienstleistungszentrum in San Maurizio d'Opaglio, Novara (1999).

Project on page 25/
Projekt Seite 25
Stop Line leisure centre/
Stop Line Freizeitzentrum
Curno, Bergamo,
Italy/Italien 1995
Collaborators/Mitarbeit:
Laura Andreini, Giovanni Polazzi, Marco Casamonti, Silvia Fabi, Nicola Santini, Giuseppe Fioroni, Antonella Dini, Michael Heffernann, Andrea Sensoli
Photographer/Foto:
Pietro Savorelli

arribas

Alfredo Arribas, born in Barcelona in 1954, graduates in architecture at ETSAB, the Barcelona Polytechnic. In 1978 he starts to lecture at the Academy, actively participating in works by the FAD (Institute for the Development of Decorative Arts), where he is appointed vice-president from 1986 to 1988. Distinguished projects realised by the Alfredo Arribas Arquitectos Asociatos studio, founded in 1986, are "Barna Crossing", a space conceived in 1989 for the Palace Hotel II in Fukuoka, Japan; the wind monument at the Plaça de Catalunya in Roses in 1990; the Spanish Pavilion at the Frankfurt Book Fair in 1991.

Alfredo Arribas wurde 1954 in Barcelona geboren und studierte Architektur an der dortigen technischen Hochschule ETSAB. Seit 1978 ist er Dozent an der Universität und Mitarbeiter des FAD

(Institut für die Entwicklung dekorativer Kunst), von 1986 bis 1988 war er Vizepräsident. Die wichtigsten der zahlreichen Projekte des 1986 gegründeten Büros Alfredo Arribas Arquitectos Asociatos sind „Barna Crossing", ein 1989 für das Palace Hotel II in Fukuoka, Japan, gestalteter Raum, das 1990 realisierte Windmonument auf der Plaça de Catalunya in Roses und der spanische Pavillon auf der Frankfurter Buchmesse im Jahr 1991.

Projects on pages 31, 41/
Projekte auf den Seiten 31, 41
Euronet Café
Frankfurt a. M., Germany/
Deutschland, 1997
Photographer/Foto:
Mihail Moldoveanu

Gran Velvet
Badalona, Barcelona,
Spain/Spanien, 1993
Photographer/Foto:
Duccio Malagamba

___

boschi
Antonello Boschi, born in Massa Marittima in 1964, graduates in architecture in Florence, 1989, where in the same year he commences his didactic activities at the Department of Furnishings and Interior Architecture chaired by Adolfo Natalini. From 1996 to 1999 he lectures on morphological characters of architecture at the same academy. His essays and projects have been published in international journals such as "Area", "Abitare", "The Architectural Review" and "World Architecture".
He not only works in design but also participates in national and international architecture competitions. In 1994 he won a prize with his project for the urban fittings of Castiglioncello.

Antonello Boschi wurde 1964 in Massa Marittima geboren, schloss 1989 sein Architekturstudium in Florenz ab und wurde Dozent an dem von Adolfo Natalini geleiteten Lehrstuhl für Innenarchitektur. Von

1996 bis 1999 nahm er dort einen Lehrauftrag für architektonische Formenlehre wahr. Seine Aufsätze und Projekte wurden in internationalen Zeitschriften wie „Area", „Abitare", „The Architectural Review" und „World Architecture" veröffentlicht.
Er ist im Bereich Design tätig und nimmt außerdem an nationalen sowie internationalen Wettbewerben teil. 1994 gewann er den Wettbewerb für die Stadtgestaltung in Castiglioncello.

Project on page 47/
Projekt Seite 47
Bar-Restaurant L'Arca
Follonica, Grosseto,
Italy/Italien, 1997
Photographer/Foto:
Alessandro Ciampi

___

branson coates architecture
Doug Branson and Nigel Coates, both from England and devoted equally to architecture and lecturing, found Branson Coates in London in 1985 with the aim of developing a multi-disciplinary approach to the architectonic project. Having realised approximately twenty projects in Japan, including three new buildings, they proceed to focus on projects in the United Kingdom, receiving a number of commissions of public character: the enlargement of the Geffrey Museum in London (1998); the realisation of the National Centre for Popular Music in Sheffield (1999); the Body Zone inside the Millennium Dome in London. Projects now underway are: Inside Out, a travelling exhibition for the British Council; a project for the Venice Biennale; and the conversion of Cureghem, an ancient college of veterinary science in Brussels, into a bio-park.

Die Engländer Doug Branson und Nigel Coates, beide sowohl als Architekten als auch in der universitären Lehre tätig, gründeten 1985 in London das Büro Branson Coates mit dem Ziel der interdisziplinären Projektierung von Bauwerken. Nach der Realisierung

von mehr als 20 Projekten in Japan, darunter drei Neubauten, konzentrieren sie sich nun auf Projekte innerhalb Großbritanniens und wurden inzwischen auch mit einigen öffentlichen Aufträgen betraut, zum Beispiel mit der Erweiterung des Geffrey Museum in London (1998), mit dem Bau des National Centre for Popular Music in Sheffield (1999) und mit der Gestaltung der Body Zone im Londoner Millennium Dome. Zu den laufenden Projekten zählen Inside Out, eine Wanderausstellung des British Council, ein Entwurf für die Biennale in Venedig und die Umwandlung des betagten tiermedizinischen Ausbildungsinstituts Cureghem in Brüssel in einen Bio-Park.

Project on page 57/
Projekt Seite 57
Bar Bargo
Glasgow, Britain/
Großbritannien, 1996
Collaborators/Mitarbeit: Allan Bell, Tony Burley, Mick Haley, Geoff Makstutis, Gerrard O'Carroll, John Paul, Oriel Prizeman, Simon Vernon Hancourt
Photographer/Foto: Phil Sayer

___

cavaglià comoglio
Gianfranco Cavaglià, born in 1945 in Turin, graduates in architecture at Turin Polytechnic. He is associate professor of technology of architecture. Focusing on living spaces and their inherent problems, he combines his studies on technology and its applications in developing countries with an interest in transformation processes, setting targets of sustainable development, even for less industrialized contexts.
He has worked on improvement schemes for living, commercial and hospital premises and fitted out shops, exhibitions and museums in Italy and abroad.

Eraldo Comoglio was born in Montanaro in 1943. Having graduated at the Faculty of Architecture at Turin Polytechnic, he and some other professionals found the Ita-

lian centre for the constructional development of rising nations.
Since 1997 he has worked with the architectural planning workshop in the Faculty of Architecture at Turin Polytechnic.
Examples of his projects: the Seguela stadium in Costa d'Avorio; the Chiesa della Risurrezione in Turin; the construction of three housing estates in Somalia; a school of restoration studies; an auditorium and a medical centre in Turin.

Gianfranco Cavaglià wurde 1945 in Turin geboren und studierte Architektur an der dortigen Technischen Hochschule. Er ist Hochschuldozent im Fach Bautechnologie. Sein Spezialgebiet ist die Problematik des Wohnens, er befasst sich vor allem mit der Frage, wie die neuen Technologien so eingesetzt werden können, dass auch in weniger industrialisierten Ländern ein bestimmtes Maß an Entwicklung und Veränderung erreicht werden kann.
Er realisierte etwa Umbauten von Wohnhäusern, Gewerbeeinheiten und Krankenhäusern und projektierte Geschäfte, Ausstellungen und Museen in Italien und in anderen Ländern.

Eraldo Comoglio wurde 1943 in Montanaro geboren. Nach seinem Studium an der Fakultät für Architektur der Technischen Hochschule Turin gründete er zusammen mit anderen Architekten das „Centro Italiano per lo sviluppo edilizio delle nazioni emergenti", eine Institution zur Förderung der baulichen Entwicklung in Schwellenländern.

Seit 1997 ist er Mitarbeiter im Fachbereich Bauprojektplanung an der Technischen Hochschule Turin.
Zu den von ihm realisierten Projekten zählen das Stadion von Seguela, Elfenbeinküste, die Chiesa della Risurrezione in Turin, drei Wohnsiedlungen in Somalia sowie eine Schule für Restauratoren, ein Konzertsaal und ein medizinisches Zentrum in Turin.

Project on page 67/
Projekt Seite 67
Giolitti Lunch & Tea
Turin, Italy/Italien, 1991
Collaborators/Mitarbeit:
Gianfranco Torri
Photographer/Foto:
Pino Dell'Aquila

cavagnari
James Cavagnari, a Londoner born in 1964, graduates in architecture in Florence in 1989 and specialises in CAD at the Visual Media Group. In 1994 he founds Prima Progetti, based in New York since 1999. Prima Progetti is a studio that focuses on interior design and the planning of spaces in commercial buildings in addition to rescuing and restoring historical buildings. Projects: the J&J hotel in Florence in 1995, the residential estate Villas del Mar in Mexico, the worldwide Salvatore Ferragamo chain of boutiques (including points of sale inside many airports). His activities for Ferragamo will be continued in future in addition to other private construction schemes such as the Postman Home loft in New York, the Schnitzer villa in Mexico and the renovation of a private yacht in Viareggio.

Der Londoner James Cavagnari, Jahrgang 1964, schloss 1989 sein Architekturstudium in Florenz ab, spezialisierte sich bei der Visual Media Group auf CAD und gründete 1994 das Büro Prima Progetti, das seit 1999 seinen Sitz in New York hat. Prima Progetti widmet sich vornehmlich dem Design von Innenräumen, der Realisierung von Gewerbeobjekten sowie der Restaurierung und Wiedernutzbarmachung von historischen Gebäuden. Zu den Projekten des Büros zählen das Hotel J&J in Florenz (1995), der Siedlungskomplex Villas del Mar in Mexiko und Filialen der Boutiquen-Kette Salvatore Ferragamo in aller Welt (darunter Läden in zahlreichen Flughäfen). Neben der Fortführung der Tätigkeit für Ferragamo sind weitere private Bauvorhaben geplant,

zum Beispiel der Loft Postman Home in New York und die Villa Schnitzer in Mexiko, sowie die Renovierung einer Privatjacht in Viareggio.

Project on page 77/
Projekt Seite 77
Club Enogastronomico
Orient-Express
Florence, Italy/
Florenz, Italien, 1998
Collaborators/Mitarbeit:
Laura Capecchi
Photographer/Foto:
Pietro Savorelli

claesson koivisto rune architects
The Claesson Koivisto Rune studio, based in Stockholm, was founded as a joint venture in 1995 between three architects: Marten Claesson, educated in Sweden and the USA; Eero Koivisto, who studied in Finland, Sweden and the USA; Ola Rune, whose studies took the architect to Sweden, Denmark and England. Their design of furnishings and accessories has attracted several significant international clients: Asplund, Boffi, Cappellini, Nola and Swedese. Latest architectonic achievements: the residence of the Swedish ambassador in Berlin (1999); the Sony Music offices in Stockholm (1999); the Gucci boutique in Stockholm (1998).

Das Büro Claesson Koivisto Rune mit Sitz in Stockholm wurde 1995 von drei Architekten gegründet: Marten Claesson, der in Schweden und den USA studierte, Eero Koivisto, den das Studium nach Finnland, Schweden und in die USA führte, und Ola Rune, der sein Studium in Schweden, Dänemark und England absolvierte. Im Bereich der Innenraumgestaltung und -ausstattung haben die drei eine Reihe illustrer Auftraggeber vorzuweisen, darunter Asplund, Boffi, Cappellini, Nola und Swedese. Zu den jüngsten Projekten gehören der Sitz des schwedischen Botschafters in Berlin (1999), die Büroräume von Sony Music in

Stockholm (1999) und die Gucci-Boutique in Stockholm (1998).

Project on page 83/
Projekt Seite 83
One Happy Cloud Restaurant
Stockholm, Sweden/
Schweden, 1997
Collaborators/Mitarbeit:
Cristiane Bosse, Mathias
Ståhlbom, Nille Svensson
Photographer/Foto:
Patrik Engquist

correa turull

After graduating from the Faculty of Architecture in Barcelona in 1992, Iñigo Correa and Federico Turull unite their professional experiences gathered during their studies under Federico Correa and Alfonso Milà, Colin St. John Wilson, Peter Eisenman and Pep Bonet-Oscar Tusquets to launch the Correa-Turull studio, based in Barcelona. The studio's activities focus on several fields, ranging from private building schemes to creating stands for various types of exhibition. Important achievements: in the private construction sector, residences in Amman; the archaeological foundation project in Sudan; Casa Sorensen on Ibiza; several building improvement schemes on Spanish territory. In the public building sector: the Olympic badminton pavilion in Barcelona; the Tarragona golf club and the Karima museum in Sudan. In the commercial sector: the Häagen-Dasz ice-cream chain; the Capucine Puerari boutique in Barcelona; the K&E clothes boutiques in Spain.

Nach dem 1992 in Barcelona abgeschlossenen Architekturstudium führten Iñigo Correa und Federico Turull ihre bei Federico Correa und Alfonso Milà, Colin St. John Wilson, Peter Eisenman und Pep Bonet-Oscar Tusquets gesammelten Berufserfahrungen im Büro Correa-Turull in Barcelona zusammen. Das vielfältige Betätigungsfeld des Büros reicht von Privatgebäuden bis hin zu Ausstellungsständen verschiedenster

Art. Zu den wichtigsten Projekten zählen im Bereich der Privatbauten Wohnsiedlungen in Amman, der Entwurf für eine archäologische Stiftung im Sudan, die Casa Sorensen auf Ibiza und zahlreiche Umbauten in Spanien. Im Bereich öffentlicher Gebäude der Badminton-Pavillon für die Olympiade in Barcelona, der Golfklub in Tarragona und das Karima-Museum im Sudan, im Bereich gewerblicher Bauten die Eiscafé-Kette Häagen-Dasz, die Boutique Capucine Puerari in Barcelona und die K&E-Bekleidungsgeschäfte in Spanien.

Project on page 91/
Projekt Seite 91
Restaurant Servicio Wilson
Barcelona, Spain/
Spanien, 1992
Photographer/Foto:
Alberto Piovano

cortes

Pepe Cortes, born in Barcelona in 1946, founds in the early seventies the design group "Grupo Abierto de Diseño", which realises the jewellery boutiques Cubic & Oriol, Werner music shop and the Poliglas offices in Barcelona. In the nineties he plans the offices for the Barcelona free-trade zone consortium and is awarded the FAD prize for the restaurant Tragaluz. Other recent achievements: the decorative design project of a private building in Spain; the "Ara és demà" exhibition commissioned by the Catalan Regional Government; a large commercial centre in Barcelona; the renovation of the gardens, the sportscentre, swimming pool and terrace bar of the Hotel Juan Carlos I.

Der 1946 in Barcelona geborene Pepe Cortes gründete Anfang der 70er Jahre die Designergruppe „Grupo Abierto de Diseño", mit der er die Juweliergeschäfte Cubic und Oriol, das Schallplattengeschäft Werner und die Poliglas-Büros in Barcelona realisierte. In den 90er Jahren entwarf er die Büros des Konsortiums der zollfreien Zone in Barcelona und er-

hielt den FAD-Preis für das Restaurant Tragaluz. Weitere Projekte jüngeren Datums sind die Innenausstattung eines Privathauses in Spanien, die Ausstellung „Ara és demà" im Auftrag der Katalanischen Regionalregierung, ein großes Einkaufszentrum in Barcelona und die Erneuerung des Parks, der Sportanlagen, des Swimmingpools und der Terrassenbar des Hotels Juan Carlos I.

Project on page 101/
Projekt Seite 101
Tragaluz Restaurant
Barcelona, Spain/Spanien, 1990
Collaborators/Mitarbeit:
Sandra Tarruella, Jesus Jimenez,
Javier Mariscal, Isabel Esteve
Photographer/Foto:
Mihail Moldoveanu

eusebi

Born in San Benedetto del Tronto in 1960, Vincenzo Eusebi graduates at the Faculty of Engineering in Ancona, and in 1999 he is awarded his Master's degree at the School of Public Administration in Rome. After graduation he alternates between the technical administration of large building sites and research projects at the Building Institute of the Faculty of Engineering in Ancona. Some of his latest works: a boutique in San Benedetto del Tronto; the plans for a gallery of contemporary art (Nespolo Foundation); the renovation of the State Hotel Management Institute; two shops; the fittings of the exhibition Mare di corda; the IPSSAR improvement and expansion scheme.

Der 1960 in San Benedetto del Tronto geborene Vincenzo Eusebi studierte an der Technischen Hochschule Ancona. 1999 erwarb er den Master-Titel an der Verwaltungshochschule in Rom. Nach seinem Studium war er sowohl als Bauleiter bei Großprojekten als auch am Institut für Bauwesen der Technischen Hochschule Ancona tätig. Zu seinen jüngsten Projekten gehören eine Boutique in San Benedetto del Tronto, ein Museum für moderne Kunst (Fondazione Nespolo), der Umbau der Staatlichen Hotelfachschule, zwei Geschäfte, die Ausstellungsarchitektur für „Mare di corda" und der Entwurf für den Umbau des Istituto Professionale di Stato per i Servizi Alberghieri e della Ristorazione (IPSSAR).

Project on page 109/
Projekt Seite 109
Bar For Love or Money
Martinsicuro, Teramo,
Italy/Italien, 1995
Photographer/Foto:
Sandro Lanciotti

fin architects
and designers inc.
Fin Architects and Designers, founded by Andy Martin in 1996 and now established in Paris and London, focus their activities on restaurants and inns, including solutions for private residential schemes and the world of television and cinema. Recent achievements, all located in London: the bar-restaurant-pub complex Mash 2; the Peyton Residence; the restaurant Isola; the Spurwell Residence.

Andy Martin, born in Sydney in 1963, studies in London. After participating in several furnishing design exhibitions in Australia, in 1992 he exhibits the Gastrula table and Halo lamp at the Salone del Mobile in Milan. Before founding his group, he realises a number of projects furnishing restaurants, bars and inns in London, Australia and Dublin.
His publications are also international in character: "Domus" in Italy; "Frame" in the Netherlands; "Elle Magazine" in Australia; "Design News" in Japan.

Das 1996 von Andy Martin gegründete Büro Fin Architects and Designers mit Niederlassungen in Paris und London ist auf Restaurants und Hotels spezialisiert, realisiert aber auch private Wohnhäuser sowie Projekte für Film und Fernsehen. Arbeiten jüngeren

Datums sind der Lokal-Komplex Mash 2, die Peyton Residence, das Restaurant Isola und die Spurwell Residence in London.

Andy Martin wurde 1963 in Sydney geboren und studierte in London. Er nahm an zahlreichen Möbeldesign-Ausstellungen in Australien teil und stellte 1992 den Tisch Gastrula und die Leuchte Halo auf dem „Salone del Mobile" in Mailand aus. Vor der Gründung des Büros entwarf er Einrichtungen für Restaurants, Bars und Hotels in London, Australien und Dublin.
Auch das Spektrum der Zeitschriften, in denen er publizierte, ist international: „Domus" in Italien, „Frame" in Holland, „Elle Magazine" in Australien und „Design News" in Japan.

Project on page 119/
Projekt Seite 119
Isola Restaurant
London, Britain/
Großbritannien, 1999
Collaborators/Mitarbeit:
Andy Martin, Simon Shaw
Photographer/Foto:
Nick Kane

foster and partners
Norman Foster, born in Manchester in 1935, studies at the university in his home town, completing his academic career with a Master's degree from Yale. In 1967 he founds the studio Foster Associates, when goes on to gain worldwide fame as Foster and Partners; since then he has received over 190 international awards and won more than 50 national and international competitions.
His great achievements are located all over the globe, his most representative being the new Reichstag in Berlin, the Great Court for the British Museum in London, the Metropolitano in Bilbao, the American Air Museum in Duxford, England, Hong Kong International Airport, and the Millennium Bridge in London. Foster and his collaborators have always shown a keen interest in city planning and the infrastructure of communication.

Foster's activity is studded with prizes and awards of the highest order, the most recent being a life peerage conferred by Queen Elizabeth in 1999.

Der 1935 in Manchester geborene Norman Foster studierte Architektur an der Universität seiner Heimatstadt und schloss seine Ausbildung mit dem Master-Titel in Yale ab. 1967 gründete er das Büro Foster Associates, das dann weltweit als Foster and Partners bekannt wurde. Seither hat er über 190 internationale Auszeichnungen erhalten und über 50 nationale und internationale Wettbewerbe gewonnen. 1999 wurde er von Königin Elisabeth zum Lord ernannt.
Seine Projekte sind über die ganze Welt verstreut. Zu nennen sind vor allem der neue Reichstag in Berlin, der Great Court für das British Museum in London, die Metro in Bilbao, das American Air Museum in Duxford, England, der internationale Flughafen von Hong Kong und die Millennium Bridge in London. Das besondere Interesse von Foster und seinen Mitarbeitern gilt seit je der Städteplanung und den Problemen einer menschengerechten Infrastruktur.

Project on page 133/
Projekt Seite 133
Reichstag Restaurant
The New German Parliament/
Restaurant im Reichstag
Neues deutsches Parlamentsgebäude, Berlin,
Germany/Deutschland, 1999
Collaborators/Mitarbeit:
David Nelson, Mark Braun,
Mark Sutcliffe, Christian
Hallmann, Ulrich Hamann,
Dieter Muller, Ingo Pott
Photographer/Foto:
Nigel Young, Dennis Gilbert

freixes miranda varis
arquitectes sl.
Daniel Freixes Melero was born in Barcelona in 1946, where he lives and works. His professional career as an architect is accompanied by his university lecturing duties. His

achievements range from fitting exhibitions and museums of architecture to interior design. With Vicente Miranda, Eulalia Gonzáles, Pep Angli and Vicenç Bou he establishes Varis Arquitectes, which leads to a joint venture lasting fifteen years.
A few of his achievements: in Barcelona, Colt Park (FAD prize in 1976); the Ramon Llull Faculty of Communications Sciences; Zsa-Zsa Bar (FAD prize in 1989); Selz Bar (FAD prize in 1992); in Girona, the Tomas Mallol Cine Collection Museum; in Madrid, the Nodo Restaurant; in Seville, the Terra exhibition in the Sailing Pavilion at Expo '92; in Berlin Dietrich's Bar at the Grand Hyatt Hotel.

Daniel Freixes Melero wurde 1946 in Barcelona geboren, wo er noch heute lebt und arbeitet. Neben seiner beruflichen Tätigkeit lehrt er auch an der Universität. Er realisierte Ausstellungs- und Museumseinrichtungen, Gebäude und Innenräume. Seit 15 Jahren arbeitet er unter dem Label Varis Arquitectes mit Vicente Miranda, Eulalia Gonzáles, Pep Angli und Vicenç Bou zusammen.

Zu seinen Projekten zählen der Colt Park (FAD-Preis 1976), die Ramon Llull Faculty of Communications Sciences, die Zsa-Zsa Bar (FAD-Preis 1989) und die Selz Bar (FAD-Preis 1992) in Barcelona, das Tomas Mallol Cine Collection Museum in Girona, das Restaurant Nodo in Madrid, die Ausstellung Terra im Seefahrt-Pavillon der Expo '92 in Sevilla sowie die Dietrich's Bar des Grand Hyatt Hotels in Berlin.

Projects on pages 139, 147, 159/
Projekte auf den Seiten 139, 147, 159
freixes varis arquitectes sl.
Dietrich's Bar
Berlin, Germany/
Deutschland, 1999
Collaborators/Mitarbeit:
Vicente Miranda, Vicenç Bou,
Eulalia González
Photographer/Foto:
Mihail Moldoveanu

freixes varis arquitectes sl.
Nodo Restaurant/
Restaurant Nodo
Madrid, Spain/Spanien, 1998
Collaborators/Mitarbeit:
Vicente Miranda, Vicenç Bou,
Eulalia González
Photographer/Foto:
Mihail Moldoveanu

freixes miranda
Zsa-Zsa Bar
Barcelona, Spain/Spanien, 1989
Collaborators/Mitarbeit:
Marta Bosch, Eulalia González
Photographer/Foto:
Mihail Moldoveanu

hadid
Zaha Hadid is a designer and architect who has turned her activities in teaching and research into her own personal mission for uncompromising modernism. After studying architecture in London she starts her teaching career, obtaining prestigious chairs such as the Kenzo Tange Chair at Harvard, the Sullivan Chair at Chicago, and various visiting professor positions in the USA and Europe. Parallel to these activities she successfully participates in a number of international competitions, always basing her projects on research. Some of her latest projects: the Centro Arti Contemporanee in Rome in 1999; the skiing trampoline in Innsbruck in the same year; large-scale urban studies for the cities of Hamburg, Madrid, Bordeaux and Cologne in addition to solutions for museums in Austria, Spain, England and Quatar. The publications and monographs dedicated to her, prestigious exhibitions, the last one being at the MoMA in San Francisco in 1997–1998, as well as permanent exhibitions, also at the MoMA and the Deutsches Architektur Museum in Frankfurt, round off the brief portrait of this extremely active and eclectic designer.

Die Designerin und Architektin Zaha Hadid hat sich in Beruf, Lehre und Forschung einem kom-

promisslosen Modernismus verschrieben. Stationen ihrer nach dem Architekturstudium in London aufgenommenen Lehrtätigkeit waren renommierte Lehrstühle wie der Kenzo Tange Chair in Harvard und der Sullivan Chair in Chicago sowie Gastprofessuren in den USA und in Europa. Gleichzeitig nahm sie auf der Basis ihrer Forschungen mit Erfolg an zahlreichen internationalen Wettbewerben teil. Projekte jüngeren Datums sind das Centro Arti Contemporanee in Rom (1999), die Sprungschanze in Innsbruck (1999), groß angelegte städtebauliche Studien für Hamburg, Madrid, Bordeaux und Köln sowie Entwürfe für Museen in Österreich, Spanien, England und Katar. Das Engagement und die vielseitigen Arbeiten der Architektin wurden in Publikationen, Monographien, Retrospektiven (zuletzt 1997–1998 im MoMA in San Francisco) und ständigen Ausstellungen (ebenfalls im MoMA und im Deutschen Architektur Museum in Frankfurt am Main) gewürdigt.

Project on page 167/
Projekt Seite 167
Moonsoon Restaurant & Bar
Sapporo, Japan, 1990
Collaborators/Mitarbeit:
Bill Goodwin, Shin Egashira,
Kar Hwa Ho, Edgar Gonzales,
Brian Langlands, Ed Gaskin,
Yuko Moriyama, Urit Luden,
Craig Kiner, Dianne Hunter-
Gorman, Patrik Schumacher,
Michael Wolfson, Satoshi
Ohashi, David Gomersall,
Daniel Chadwick
Photographer/Foto:
Paul Warchol Inc., Nacasa &
Partners Inc., Edward Woodman

jakob macfarlane
Dominique Jakob, the French architect, and the American Brendan MacFarlane, set up the studio Jakob+MacFarlane Sarl d'architecture in Paris. Their accomplishments are born out by the quantity and prestigious nature of the projects they work on.
Some of their latest projects: Restaurant Georges, illustrated here,

in the Centre Pompidou in Paris (2000); in the private building sector, the attic storey of the Maison T, a residence realised at La Garenne Colombes in 1994 by a private client. Both architects are active lecturers at higher institutes of architecture in France, currently working on a series of ambitious projects and international contests, outstanding examples of which are the renovation of theatre and banquet halls.

Der französische Architekt Dominique Jakob und der Amerikaner Brendan MacFarlane haben der Firma Jakob+MacFarlane Sarl d'architecture in Paris ihren Namen gegeben. Quantität und Qualität seiner Entwürfe zeichnen das Büro aus.
Zu den neuesten Projekten zählen das in diesem Band abgebildete Restaurant Georges im Centre Pompidou in Paris (2000) und das Dachgeschoss der Maison T, eines 1994 für einen privaten Auftraggeber in La Garenne Colombes realisierten Wohnhauses. Beide Architekten lehren außerdem an Architekturhochschulen in Frankreich und arbeiten zurzeit an einer Reihe von ehrgeizigen Projekten und internationalen Wettbewerben, vor allem im Bereich des Umbaus von Theater- und Festsälen.

Project on page 183/
Projekt Seite 183
Restaurant Georges
Centre Georges Pompidou,
Paris, France/Frankreich, 2000
Photographer/Foto:
Mihail Moldoveanu

lazzarini pickering
Claudio Lazzarini, born in Rome in 1953, graduates in architecture at La Sapienza University and Carl Pickering, born in Sydney in 1960, emigrates to Italy in 1980 and graduates in architecture in Venice. In 1983 they start their collaboration.
Their studio operates in Italy and abroad, conducting architectonic projects of recovery and reno-

vation, design and artistic supervision.
Their most recent projects include the renovation of villas in Tuscany, Sicily and Capri, apartments in Rome and Monte Carlo, the realisation of the Fendi boutique in Milan. Lazzarini and Pickering have been responsible for over 180 projects for international trade fairs, shops, gardens and boat interiors in Italy, the USA, Japan and Brazil. In 1999 two prestigious international prizes went to their project for the interiors of a carbon-fibre vessel, 34 metres long, commissioned by Wally Yachts, a revolutionary concept for the design of sailing boat interiors.
The works by Lazzarini and Pickering are acknowledged accordingly in international architecture and interior design publications.

Claudio Lazzarini, der 1953 in Rom geboren wurde und an der dortigen Universität La Sapienza Architektur studierte, und Carl Pickering, der 1960 in Sydney geboren wurde, 1980 nach Italien kam und in Venedig Architektur studierte, arbeiten seit 1983 zusammen.
Der Tätigkeitsbereich des Büros umfasst Neubauten, Restaurierungen und Sanierungen, Design und künstlerische Beratung.
Zu den jüngsten Projekten zählen die Restaurierung von Villen in der Toskana, auf Sizilien und Capri, Wohnungen in Rom und Monte Carlo sowie die Fendi-Boutique in Mailand. Darüber hinaus realisierten Lazzarini und Pickering über 180 Projekte für internationale Messen, Geschäfte, Gartenanlagen und Schiffsausstattungen in Italien, den USA, Japan und Brasilien. 1999 wurde ihr von Wally Yachts in Auftrag gegebener, revolutionärer Entwurf für die Innenräume eines 34 Meter langen Schiffs aus Kohlenstofffasern mit zwei internationalen Preisen ausgezeichnet.
Die Werke von Lazzarini und Pickering wurden in zahlreichen internationalen Publikationen zu Architektur und Innenraumgestaltung gewürdigt.

Project on page 193/
Projekt Seite 193
nil Bar e Ristorante
Rome, Italy/Rom, Italien, 1997
Collaborators/Mitarbeit:
Giuseppe Postet, Fabio Sonnino
Photographer/Foto:
Matteo Piazza

mecanoo architecten
Mecanoo studio was founded in 1984 in Delft, the Netherlands, by Henk Doll, the Dutch architect and Francine Houben, who both graduated in 1984. In the first few years of its activities the studio focused on building projects in Dutch urban areas in need of renovation. But since 1987, the year it was awarded the Rotterdam Maaskant prize for young architects, it has extended its field of operations, increasing its staff to about 55, to develop a complex approach: polyfunctional buildings and integral urban projects which combine city and landscape planning, architecture and interior design.
Two of its many projects: in 1997 the library at Delft Polytechnic received the national Steelprize, and the National Heritage Museum in Arnhem opened its doors to the public in May 2000.

Das Büro Mecanoo wurde von den Niederländern Henk Doll und Francine Houben nach Abschluss ihres Architekturstudiums 1984 in Delft gegründet. In den ersten Jahren arbeiteten sie hauptsächlich an städtebaulichen Sanierungsprojekten in den Niederlanden. Nachdem sie 1987 den Rotterdam-Maaskant-Preis für junge Architekten erhalten hatten, stockten sie ihren Mitarbeiterstab auf 55 Personen auf und spezialisierten sich auf komplexe Entwürfe für Multifunktionsgebäude und groß angelegte städtebauliche Projekte, bei denen Stadt- und Landschaftsplanung, Architektur und Innenraumgestaltung zusammenwirken.
Zu den zahlreichen von Mecanoo realisierten Projekten gehören die Bibliothek der Technischen Hochschule Delft, die 1997 mit dem

niederländischen Steelprize ausgezeichnet wurde, und das National Heritage Museum in Arnheim, das im Mai 2000 offiziell eröffnet wurde.

Project on page 207/
Projekt Seite 207
Brasserie Blauw
Delft, the Netherlands/
Niederlande, 1999
Collaborators/Mitarbeit:
Francine Houben,
Alfa Hügelmann, Carlo Bevers,
Henk Bouwer, Maaike Bruins,
Tom Grootscholten,
Angelique Wisse
Photographer/Foto:
Christian Richters

miás pla salló
Josep Miás Gifre, born in Banyoles in 1967, has worked at Enric Miralles' studio since 1991. Two of his most significant achievements are the bar at the Banyoles swimming pool and the Solius sports centre.

Francesc Pla Ferrer, born in Barcelona in 1968, worked at Enric Miralles' studio from 1990 to 1994. He is currently working together with Josep Bohigas and Iñaki Baquero (Bopba arquitectos). Some of his most representative works are the fittings for an exhibition on Andrea Palladio, an exhibition for Hermés, a hotel in Bilbao and an exhibition area for artistic glass.

Josep Salló Colell, architect, born in Girona in 1962, was commissioned with the construction and carpentry of the Tubo Bar.

Der 1967 in Banyoles geborene Josep Miás Gifre ist seit 1991 Mitarbeiter bei Enric Miralles. Zu seinen wichtigsten Projekten zählen die Bar im Schwimmbad von Banyoles und das Sportzentrum in Solius.

Francesc Pla Ferrer wurde 1968 in Barcelona geboren und war von 1990 bis 1994 im Büro von Enric Miralles tätig. Zurzeit ist er Mitarbeiter von Josep Bohigas und Iña-

ki Baquero (Bopba arquitectos). Zu seinen bedeutendsten Werken gehören eine Ausstellung über Andrea Palladio, eine Ausstellung für Hermés, ein Hotel in Bilbao und ein Ausstellungsraum für Glaskunst.

Der Architekt Josep Salló Colell, 1962 in Girona geboren, entwarf die Architektur und die Holzkonstruktionen für die Tubo Bar.

Project on page 217/
Projekt Seite 217
Tubo Bar
Barcelona, Spain/
Spanien, 1993
Collaborators/Mitarbeit:
Albert Ribera, Higini Aran,
David Garcia, Miquel Llorenz
Photographer/Foto:
Duccio Malagamba

micheli
Simone Micheli founds the architecture studio with the same name in 1990. He wins several architecture and design competitions in Europe, drafting plans for objects, for exhibition fittings, houses, hotels, shops and offices. He supervises experimental exhibition events for a number of the most significant international trade fairs: Brussels, Genoa, Milan, Rome, Verona, Tokio. Since 1998 he has been editor-in-chief of the annual "Contract International Guide" and, in 2000, he is visiting professor at the Hong Ik University of Seoul.
He realises projects for Alcatel Italia, Cerruti, Illy, Marzotto, Montedison, Kronenbourg, Peroni, Perugina, Poste Italiane, Toyota, among others.

Simone Micheli gründete 1990 das gleichnamige Architekturbüro. Er gewann verschiedene Architektur- und Designwettbewerbe in Europa, und hat Objekte, Ausstellungsarchitekturen, Häuser, Hotels, Geschäfte und Büros entworfen. Er entwirft experimentelle Ausstellungs-Events für einige der wichtigsten internationalen Messen: Brüssel, Genua, Mailand,

Rom, Verona, Tokio. Seit 1998 ist er Herausgeber des Jahrbuchs „Contract International Guide". Im Jahr 2000 hat er eine Gastprofessur an der Hong Ik Universität in Seoul.
Er realisiert unter anderem Projekte für Alcatel Italia, Cerruti, Illy, Marzotto, Montedison, Kronenbourg, Peroni, Perugina, die italienische Post und Toyota.

Project on page 223/
Projekt Seite 223
Peroni Music Café
Castelfranco Veneto, Treviso,
Italy/Italien, 1999
Collaborators/Mitarbeit: Luca
Bolognese, Cristina Lombardi,
Silvia Scuffi Abati
Photographer/Foto:
Cozzi e Scribani

monti muti
Claudio Monti, after studying architecture in Venice and working with the studios Citterio & Sottsass e Associati, founds Studiomonti in 1998 with two partners. The studio has realised and currently continues to realise projects for houses, shops, public building premises and trade fair fittings in Italy and abroad, for example the Rauenstein Restaurant in Vienna, the fittings for the Pitti Immagine Uomo, various showrooms and shops for Corneliani, the new corporate identity (with studio Citterio) for the oil company Tamoil.

Francesco Muti, born in Florence, graduates in architecture at Milan Polytechnic in 1996. In 1997 he designs the new DC14 for the Della Pasqua shipyard in Ravenna. In 1998 he joins studio Teprin in Ravenna, where he continues his architectural and urban planning activities.
One of his most important experiences is his participation in the planning and execution of the "Parco Teodorico" in Ravenna with studio Teprin & Boris Prodecca. Together with Claudio Monti he realises Armani Luxottica Mido '99 and the new Studiomonti office in piazza Sant'Erasmo, Milan.

Nach seinem Architekturstudium in Venedig und der Mitarbeit in den Büros Citterio & Sottsass e Associati gründete Claudio Monti 1998 mit zwei Partnern das Büro Studiomonti. Zu seinen Projekten zählen Häuser, Geschäfte, öffentliche Gebäude und Messe-Ausstattungen in Italien und im Ausland, darunter das Restaurant Rauenstein in Wien, die Ausstattung von Pitti Immagine Uomo, verschiedene Showrooms und Boutiquen für Corneliani sowie die (zusammen mit dem Büro Citterio realisierte) neue Corporate Identity der Mineralölgesellschaft Tamoil.

Francesco Muti wurde in Florenz geboren und schloss sein Architekturstudium 1996 an der Technischen Hochschule Mailand ab. 1997 entwarf er für die Werft Della Pasqua in Ravenna das Design für die neue DC14. Seit 1998 ist er Mitarbeiter des Büros Teprin in Ravenna, wo er in den Bereichen Bauprojektplanung und Städtebau tätig ist.

Er war maßgeblich an der Planung und Realisierung des Parco Teodorico in Ravenna durch das Büro Teprin und Boris Prodecca beteiligt. Mit Claudio Monti realisierte er Armani Luxottica Mido '99 und das neue Gebäude von Studiomonti an der Piazza Sant'Erasmo in Mailand.

Project on page 235/
Projekt Seite 235
Restaurant Blu Sonora
Milano Marittima, Ravenna, Italy/Italien, 1999
Collaborators/Mitarbeit:
Silvia Tonini, Paolo Castagnetti
Photographer/Foto:
Alessandro Ciampi

morphosis
Founded by Thom Mayne in 1972, studio Morphosis has approximately twenty collaborators coordinated by Mayne himself and Kim Groves. Mayne, a graduate of the University of Southern California, is currently teaching at the UCLA

and abroad. Morphosis' projects, the subject of 18 monographs, include the Hypo Bank offices in Austria, the oncological centre Cedar's Sinai in Los Angeles and various projects in the public sector in the USA, e.g. university buildings and the Federal Court of Oregon; Morphosis has also recently been awarded the commission to build a bridge monument for the city of Los Angeles.

Das 1972 von Thom Mayne gegründete Büro Morphosis beschäftigt etwa 20 Mitarbeiter unter der Leitung von Mayne und Kim Groves. Mayne, der an der University of Southern California studierte, lehrt zurzeit an der UCLA und ist international auch an anderen Hochschulen tätig. Zu den Projekten von Morphosis, denen 18 Monographien gewidmet sind, zählen die Büros der Hypo-Bank in Österreich, das Krebsforschungszentrum Cedar's Sinai in Los Angeles und öffentliche Gebäude in den USA, darunter verschiedene Universitätsgebäude und der Federal Court in Oregon. Vor kurzem gewann Morphosis den Wettbewerb für ein Brückendenkmal in Los Angeles.

Project on page 245/
Projekt Seite 245
Tsunami
Las Vegas, Nevada, USA, 2000
Collaborators/Mitarbeit:
Kim Groves, David Rindlaub, Simon Businger, Josh Coggeshall, Jerome Daksiewicz, Manish Desai, Martin Josst, Ung Joo Scott Lee, Devin McConley
Photographer/Foto:
Farshid Assassi

nardi
Claudio Nardi, born in Prato in 1951, graduates in architecture in 1978. His professional experience begins in 1971 at the International Design showroom in Florence, subsequently built in 1975, in collaboration with the project conceived by Carlo Scarpa. His studio in Florence, currently comprising approximately twenty staff, main-

ly focuses on the planning of interiors, residential and commercial buildings in Italy and abroad, on town planning schemes. Research and continual experimentation with materials, stimulated by frequent work trips all over the world have given birth to a rich and articulate repertoire, which he deploys in his approach to architectural themes of diverging characteristics and complexities.

Claudio Nardi wurde 1951 in Prato geboren und schloss 1978 sein Architekturstudium ab. Seine Karriere begann bereits 1971 mit dem Showroom des International Design in Florenz, den er 1975 nach dem Entwurf von Carlo Scarpa realisierte. Sein Büro in Florenz, das zurzeit etwa 20 Mitarbeiter beschäftigt, befasst sich vornehmlich mit der Planung von Innenräumen, Wohn- und Geschäftsgebäuden in Italien und im Ausland sowie mit städtebaulichen Projekten. Durch das Experimentieren mit neuartigen Materialien, für das die häufigen Auslandsaufenthalte Anregungen liefern, verfügt Nardi über ein reichhaltiges und vielfältiges Repertoire, mit dem er die verschiedensten baulichen Konzepte umsetzt.

Project on page 253/
Projekt Seite 253
Bar Universo
Universo Sporting Center
Prato, Italy/Italien, 1993
Collaborators/Mitarbeit:
Leopoldo Vezzoni, Kazuyuki Toyoda, Hilary Hubbard
Photographer/Foto:
Mario Ciampi

nouvel
Jean Nouvel, born in 1945, is the co-founder of the "Mars 1976" movement, the winner of the Grand Prix d'Architecture (1987) and the prize for the best French building, the Institut du Monde Arabe, in 1987. In 1988 he joins forces with the Swiss architect Emmanuel Cattani.

His latest projects: the Poulain plant in Blois (1991), the Les Thermes hotel in Dax (1992), the opera house in Lyons (1993). Currently in the construction or planning phases: a large commercial centre in Lille, the "Tour sans fin" at the Défense in Paris, residential buildings in Düsseldorf, TV studios in Rotterdam.

Der 1945 geborene Jean Nouvel ist Mitbegründer der Bewegung „Mars 1976", Träger des Grand Prix d'Architecture (1987) und des Preises für das beste Gebäude in Frankreich, den er für den 1987 realisierten Bau des Institut du Monde Arabe erhielt. Seit 1988 arbeitet er mit dem Schweizer Architekten Emmanuel Cattani zusammen.
Zu seinen jüngsten Projekten zählen das Poulain-Werk in Blois (1991), das Hotel Les Thermes in Dax (1992) und das Opernhaus in Lyon (1993). Zurzeit arbeitet Nouvel an einem großen Handelszentrum in Lille, der „Tour sans fin" im Pariser Stadtviertel Défense, Wohnhäusern in Düsseldorf und Fernsehstudios in Rotterdam.

Project on page 263/
Projekt Seite 263
Brasserie Schutzenberger
Strasbourg, France/
Straßburg, Frankreich, 2000
Collaborators/Mitarbeit:
Alain Bony, Hubert Tonka, Marie Najdovski, Viviane Morteau, Gunther Domenig
Photographer/Foto:
Mihail Moldoveanu

ogawa depardon

The studio Ogawa/Depardon Architects, founded in 1987 by Kathryn Ogawa and Gilles Depardon, has a multi-national base, fusing the experiences of three continents, featuring a multi-disciplinary structure that aims to offer the client a full range of services in urban, architectural and interior design. Over thirty projects have been realised to date, including private building projects as well as institutional and commercial schemes. The common approach deployed in all the commissions is a gradual synergy between the architects and the client in every creative and executive phase, the studio taking meticulous care of the client's requirements and the specific features of every individual project.

Das 1987 von Kathryn Ogawa und Gilles Depardon gegründete Büro Ogawa/Depardon Architects vereinigt Erfahrungen aus drei Kontinenten und verfolgt den Anspruch, dem Kunden das gesamte Spektrum an Dienstleistungen zu bieten – von der Städteplanung über die Projektierung von Bauten bis hin zur Innenarchitektur. Bisher wurden über 30 private, öffentliche und gewerbliche Bauten realisiert. Grundlage ist eine genaue Analyse der individuellen Bedürfnisse und der kontinuierliche Austausch mit dem Auftraggeber in jeder Phase der Planung und Ausführung.

Project on page 275/
Projekt Seite 275
Bar 89
New York, USA, 1995
Collaborators/Mitarbeit:
Tuck Choeng, Mark Hage, Michael Ashkenazi
Photographer/Foto:
Mihail Moldoveanu

pallí vert

Robert Pallí Vert's studio, based in Barcelona, specialises in interior design projects, such as restaurants, shops, art galleries and industrial buildings (Jotun Paint, KPMG in Barcelona). Some of the studio's works: the restaurants Nostrus and Tio Tapas; the art gallery Art Box; the café Bagel's; the projects for Dunkin Donuts; Canal Satelite Digital; and Nani Marquina.

Die Tätigkeit des Büros von Robert Pallí Vert in Barcelona umfasst sowohl die Gestaltung von Innenräumen, Restaurants, Geschäften und Kunstgalerien als auch die Projektierung von Industriebauten (Jotun Paint, KPMG in Barcelona). Realisiert wurden unter anderem die Restaurants Nostrus und Tio Tapas, die Kunstgalerie Art Box, das Café Bagel's, Projekte für Dunkin Donuts, Canal Satelite Digital und Nani Marquina.

Project on page 283/
Projekt Seite 283
Restaurant El Racó
Barcelona, Spain/Spanien, 1999
Collaborators/Mitarbeit:
Miguel Ordoñez
Photographer/Foto:
Duccio Malagamba

rundell & associates ltd.

Mike Rundell sets up a studio of associates in London in 1994 after being active for many years as an artist in London, Barcelona and Saint Petersburg. Due to his experience as a construction expert, he pays particular care to the link between plan and reality; this permits him to glean from the history of the building to be renovated and converted its salient features so as to combine the best elements from its past with a final, completely new result. Achievements such as the Pharmacy restaurant in London and Chaikovski's apartment in Saint Petersburg, copiously illustrated in international publications, reveal the special significance of this creative and practical approach to architecture.
Further projects include the White Cube Gallery, new installations at the Tate Gallery and several residential schemes. Two currently underway are the renovation of terraced areas in Saint Petersburg and a museum in Notting Hill Gate, London.

Nach langjähriger künstlerischer Tätigkeit in London, Barcelona sowie Sankt Petersburg gründete Mike Rundell 1994 ein Gemeinschaftsbüro in London. Seine Erfahrung als Ingenieur schärfte sein Bewusstsein für das Verhältnis zwischen Entwurf und Realität: Er greift auf die Geschichte des Bauwerks zurück, mit dessen Restaurierung oder Umbau er betraut ist, um dessen wichtigste Merkmale in ein völlig neues Objekt zu integrieren. Projekte wie das Restaurant Pharmacy in London und die Wohnung von Tschaikowsky in Sankt Petersburg, beide ausführlich publiziert, veranschaulichen diese zugleich kreative und pragmatische Auseinandersetzung mit der Architektur.

Weitere bereits realisierte Projekte sind die White Cube Gallery, neue Einbauten in die Tate Gallery und zahlreiche Wohngebäude. Derzeit in Arbeit befindliche Projekte sind die Erneuerung von Terrassenanlagen in Sankt Petersburg und ein Museum in Notting Hill Gate, London.

Project on page 289/
Projekt Seite 289
Pharmacy Restaurant & Bar
London, Britain/
Großbritannien, 1998
Collaborators/Mitarbeit:
Fergus McMahon, Jackie Pastina, Bill Fancourt, Clifford Jones
Photographer/Foto: Steve White

---

santachiara
Denis Santachiara, born in 1950, starts his career as a designer by considering the linguistic potential of new technologies and the consequent aesthetic developments in the industrial sphere, realising works located between art and design. He has exhibited at the Venice Biennale, the Documenta 8 in Kassel, the National Museum of Modern Art in Tokio, the Triennale in Milan, the Quadriennale in Rome.
In 1984 he conceives and organises the exhibition "La neomerce, Il design dell'invenzione e dell'estasi artificiale", a manifesto of the branch, at the Triennale in Milan and the Centre Pompidou in Paris in addition to "I segni dell'habitat", held in Paris, Amsterdam and Barcelona.
Important works: the project for the interiors of Chartreuse de Villeneuve-lès-Avignon (1988–1992); the Musée de la Magie (1993); the fittings for Toyama square in Ja-

pan (1994–1995); the interiors of the art'otel in Dresden. In 1996 he won the international competition ZIP for the city of Saarbrücken and he designed the fittings for the New-Persona at the Florence Biennale. In 1998 he supervised the project for a new telematic banking system for the "Assicurazioni Generali" group and, by contrast, he also designed a children's play animal for the French Minister of Culture.

Denis Santachiara, geboren 1950, begann seine Karriere als Designer, wobei er sich mit den Ausdrucksmöglichkeiten neuer industrieller Technologien und den daraus resultierenden ästhetischen Entwicklungen auseinandersetzte. Er schuf Werke zwischen Kunst und Design, die auf der Biennale in Venedig, auf der Documenta 8 in Kassel, im Nationalen Museum of Modern Art in Tokio, auf der Triennale in Mailand und auf der Quadriennale in Rom ausgestellt wurden.
1984 entwarf und organisierte er die programmatische Ausstellung, die unter dem Titel „La neomerce, Il design dell'invenzione e dell'estasi artificiale" auf der Triennale in Mailand und im Pariser Centre Pompidou gezeigt wurde, sowie „I segni dell'habitat", eine Ausstellung in Paris, Amsterdam und Barcelona.
Zu den von ihm realisierten Projekten zählen die Innenräume der Chartreuse de Villeneuve-lès-Avignon (1988–1992), das Musée de la Magie in Blois (1993), die Platzgestaltung in Toyama, Japan (1994–1995) und die Innenräume des art'otel in Dresden. 1996 gewann er den internationalen Wettbewerb des Zentrums für innovative Produktion (ZIP) der Stadt Saarbrücken und entwarf die Installation The New-Persona für die Biennale in Florenz. Im Jahr 1998 war er mit der Ausarbeitung eines neuen elektronischen Banksystems für den Konzern „Assicurazioni Generali" betraut und entwickelte im Auftrag des französischen Kulturministers ein Spieltier für Kinder.

Project on page 305/
Projekt Seite 305
Epsilon Discotheque/
Diskothek Epsylon
Reggio Emilia, Italy/Italien, 1989
Photographer/Foto: Miro Zagnoli

sapey
Teresa Sapey, born in Cuneo in 1962, graduates from the Faculty of Architecture at Turin University in 1985; she then decides to complete her academic career with a Master's degree at Parson's School of Design in Paris, to dedicate herself to the pursuit of her artistic interests. After returning to Turin in 1988, she begins working with Professor Roggero, subsequently moving to Rome to continue her studies due to a joint project with the La Villette Faculty of Architecture in Paris. She goes on to specialise in the design and ergonomics of work spaces, taking advantage of the opportunity to collaborate with the designers Alberto Pinto and Jacques Garcia. In 1989 she takes part in the first world congress on the architecture of commercial work spaces, held in Sweden. In 1990 she moves to Madrid to work as an architect in Spain, briefly co-operating with Rafael de la Hoz before setting up the Estudio de Arquitectura Teresa Sapey, specialised in avant-garde design for houses, shops, restaurants and decorative objects.
Recent works: the mobile bar for Absolut Vodka; the renovation of the Bulgari and Smikke shops; a photographic installation for Tag-Heuer; the furnishing line "pastamania" for Ikea; the design of a kindergarten for Walt Disney.

Teresa Sapey wurde 1962 in Cuneo geboren, schloss 1985 ihr Architekturstudium an der Universität Turin ab und erwarb anschließend den Master-Titel an der Parson's School of Design in Paris, um eine künstlerische Laufbahn einzuschlagen. 1988 kehrte sie nach Turin zurück, wurde Mitarbeiterin von Professor Roggero und setzte dann im Rahmen eines

Projekts in Zusammenarbeit mit der Fakultät für Architektur La Villette in Paris ihre Ausbildung in Rom fort. Sie spezialisierte sich auf Design und die Ergonomie von Arbeitsplätzen und arbeitete mit den Designern Alberto Pinto und Jacques Garcia zusammen. 1989 nahm sie am ersten internationalen Kongress zur Architektur gewerblicher Arbeitsplätze in Schweden teil. Seit 1990 ist sie in Madrid als Architektin tätig, war kurze Zeit Mitarbeiterin von Rafael de la Hoz und gründete dann das Estudio de Arquitectura Teresa Sapey für avantgardistisches Design von Häusern, Geschäften, Restaurants und Einrichtungsgegenständen.
Zu den Projekten jüngeren Datums zählen eine mobile Bar für Absolut Vodka, der Umbau von Geschäften für Bulgari und Smikke, eine Fotoinstallation für Tag-Heuer, die Ikea-Einrichtungsserie „pasta-mania" und ein Kindergarten für Walt Disney.

Project on page 317/
Projekt Seite 317
Hampton Club Bar
Madrid, Spain/Spanien, 1999
Collaborators/Mitarbeit:
Marta Melendo, Tiffany Low
Photographer/Foto: Bene Angulo

---

starck
Philippe Starck, born in Paris in 1949, a student of the Schools of Neuilly and Paris, is one of the world's most eclectic and celebrated designers. His conception of expressionist architecture fuses with an impression which he himself defines as "emotional style" that bestows on every one of his creations an unmistakable personality. Starck has been hallowed by museums all over the globe, from Paris to New York and Kyoto; he has received awards such as the Grand Prix of International Design and the Oscar of Design. Since 1979 he has created objects by the trade name of Starck Products.
On the interior design plane, one of his important projects was the

famous private suite at the Élysée Palace in Paris in 1982, requested by President Mitterand; his most recent project is the restaurant Bon. On the architectural front, besides several buildings in Japan, the control tower at Bordeaux airport in 1997 must be mentioned. Starck's design is expressed on many levels, ranging from the furnishings of the French presidential residence to decorative objects, from accessories for clients such as Alessi, Kartell, Driade, Cassina and Fiam to nautical design for Bénéteau plus every possible kind of object: from a toothbrush to a scooter, to food products.
From 1993 to 1996 he accepts the position of artistic director at Thomson Consumer Electronics; he also lectures at the Accademia Domus in Milan and at the School of Decorative Arts in Paris.

Philippe Starck, der 1949 in Paris geboren wurde und in Neuilly und Paris studierte, ist einer der wandlungsfähigsten und bekanntesten Designer der Welt. Sein expressionistisches Architekturkonzept verbindet sich mit einem Ansatz, den er selbst „emotional style" nennt und der jeder seiner Kreationen einen unverwechselbaren Charakter verleiht. Museen in aller Welt, von Paris über New York bis Kyoto, stellten Starcks Werke aus; er wurde mit Preisen wie dem Grand Prix für Industriedesign und dem Oscar für Design ausgezeichnet. Seit 1979 werden Gegenstände der Marke Starck Products hergestellt.
Im Bereich der Innenraumgestaltung realisierte er neben der berühmten, vom damaligen französischen Präsidenten Mitterrand in Auftrag gegebenen Privatwohnung im Pariser Élysée-Palast (1982) erst kürzlich das Restaurant Bon. Bei den Bauprojekten ist neben zahlreichen Gebäuden in Japan der 1997 realisierte Kontrollturm des Flughafens in Bordeaux zu nennen. Das Design von Starck findet sich in den verschiedensten Bereichen: in der Ausstattung des französischen Präsi-

dentensitzes, in Einrichtungsgegenständen und Accessoires für Auftraggeber wie Alessi, Kartell, Driade, Cassina und Fiam, in der Schiffskonstruktion von Bénéteau und bei Gegenständen jeder Art, von der Zahnbürste über Motorroller bis hin zu Lebensmitteln.
Von 1993 bis 1996 war Starck künstlerischer Leiter des Unternehmens Thomson Consumer Electronics. Außerdem lehrt er an der Accademia Domus in Mailand und an der Schule für dekorative Kunst in Paris.

Project on page 327/
Projekt Seite 327
Restaurant Bon
Paris, France/Frankreich, 2000
Photographer/Foto:
Mihail Moldoveanu

---

uda volpe
UdA (Ufficio di Architettura) is founded in 1992 in Turin by Walter Camagna, Massimiliano Camoletto and Andrea Marcante. The studio's activities range from interior design and the planning of exhibition spaces to public and private architecture, restoration work and the conversion of urban spaces.

As a result of UdA's vast experience and interdisciplinary collaboration with many professionals, its focus is on living space themes, the image of commercial and public spaces, the redeployment of existing heritage buildings and industrial archaeology.
In 1998 UdA opened its second office in Milan with the studio Dell'Acqua Design.
The studio combines its professional activities with architectonic research, and participates in many competitions. Notable entries are: its restoration of the Politeama theatre in Bra (1997), which won second prize; the roof of the main entrance hall of the Molinette hospital in Turin and the additional spaces for the public (1998), for which the studio was awarded first prize; the project for the Turin section at the European 5 (1998).

Davide Volpe, born in Biella in 1966, graduates in architecture at Turin Polytechnic in 1991. In 1995 he opens his own studio in his home town Biella.

UdA (Ufficio di Architettura) wurde 1992 von Walter Camagna, Massimiliano Camoletto und Andrea Marcante in Turin gegründet. Die Tätigkeit des Büros erstreckt sich von der Innenausstattung und der Planung von Ausstellungsräumen über die Realisierung von öffentlichen und privaten Bauten bis hin zur Sanierung und Wiedernutzbarmachung städtischer Räume. Auf der Grundlage seiner vielfältigen Erfahrungen und der Zusammenarbeit mit Fachleuten anderer Disziplinen konnte sich das Büro mit der Problematik des Wohnens im Allgemeinen, der Bedeutung gewerblicher und öffentlicher Räume, der Nutzung vorhandener Bausubstanz und der Industrie-Archäologie auseinander setzen. 1998 eröffnete UdA mit dem Büro Dell'Acqua Design eine zweite Niederlassung in Mailand. Die Bemühung um neue Lösungen in der Architektur äußert sich in der Teilnahme an zahlreichen Wettbewerben: Unter anderem erhielt UdA den zweiten Preis im Wettbewerb für die Restaurierung des Politeama-Theaters in Bra (1997) sowie den ersten Preis im Wettbewerb für die Überdachung der zentralen Eingangshalle des Krankenhauses Molinette in Turin und die Besucherräume (1998) und reichte einen Entwurf für die Sektion von Turin auf der European 5 ein (1998).

Davide Volpe wurde 1966 in Biella geboren und schloss 1991 sein Architekturstudium an der Technischen Hochschule Turin ab. 1995 eröffnete er ein eigenes Büro in seiner Heimatstadt Biella.

Project on page 337/
Projekt Seite 337
Circolo La Barraca
Biella, Vercelli, Italy/
Italien, 1995
Photographer/Foto: Emilio Conti

waisbrod studio gaia
In 1995 Ilan Waisbrod storms the New York design world of restaurants, bars and hotels, winning with his Studio Gaia the prestigious James Beard Award and the commission to completely renovate the New York Palace Hotel. Waisbrod, born in Israel in 1961, studied architecture, initially at the University of Tel Aviv, then at the Milan Polytechnic.
In 1990 Waisbrod moves to the USA, winning commissions from clients such as Burlington, Elizabeth Arden, Panasonic, Nabisco and Hertz.
Some of the latest projects realised by studio Gaia: in New York, SanBox Sandwich Bars, the restaurant Caféteria, the bistro Alouette, the night club and restaurant Eugene's, the Belleclaire Hotel, the restaurant Triumph at the Iroquois Hotel, the restaurant Jimmy's Up Town.

Ilan Waisbrod nahm 1995 die New Yorker Szene für das Design von Lokalen und Hotels im Sturm, als er mit seinem Studio Gaia den begehrten James Beard Award und gleichzeitig den Auftrag für die komplette Renovierung des New York Palace Hotel erhielt. Waisbrod wurde 1961 in Israel geboren und studierte Architektur, zunächst an der Universität von Tel Aviv und dann an der Technischen Hochschule Mailand.
Seit 1990 arbeitet Waisbrod in den USA für Kunden wie Burlington, Elizabeth Arden, Panasonic, Nabisco und Hertz.
Zu den jüngsten Projekten in New York zählen die SanBox Sandwich Bars, das Restaurant Caféteria, das Bistro Alouette, der Nachtklub mit angeschlossenem Restaurant Eugene's, das Hotel Belleclaire, das Restaurant Triumph im Iroquois Hotel und das Restaurant Jimmy's Up Town.

Projects on pages 349, 361/
Projekte auf den Seiten 349, 361
Bondst Japanese Restaurant
New York, USA, 1998
Photographer/Foto:
David Joseph

23 Michael Jordan Restaurant
Chapel Hill, North Carolina,
USA, 1999
Photographer/Foto:
Mark Ballogg

windbichler
Irmfried Windbichler, born in 1947 in Kitzbühel, graduates in the Academy of Architecture in Graz, Austria. His activities focus mainly on Austria and Germany, a centre for the University clinic of Graz (1999) and a centre for handicapped people at Pischelsdorf (1999 to 2000). His participation in exhibitions, however, takes him much further afield internationally, to Cuma 4000 in Naples, for example, and his capacity as a lecturer and university language assistant to the University of Edinburgh and the New Jersey Institute of Technology in the USA.

Irmfried Windbichler wurde 1947 in Kitzbühel geboren und studierte an der Universität Graz. Er ist vornehmlich in Österreich und Deutschland tätig, wo er auch seine jüngsten Projekte realisierte: ein Gebäudekomplex für die Universitätsklinik Graz (1999) und ein Behindertenzentrum in Pischelsdorf (1999–2000). Sein internationaler Ruf gründet sich auf die Teilnahme an Ausstellungen, darunter Cuma 4000 in Neapel, und seine Lehrtätigkeit an der Universität Edinburgh und am New Jersey Institute of Technology in den USA.

Project on page 373/
Projekt Seite 373
Bar Nachtexpress
Graz, Austria/Österreich, 1990
Collaborators/Mitarbeit:
Gerhard Kuebel
Photographer/Foto:
Irmfried Windbichler

**Photographic references /
Fotonachweis**
Bene Angulo, Madrid
Farshid Assassi, Santa Barbara
Mark Ballogg, Steinkamp/Ballogg Photography, Chicago
Alessandro Ciampi, Prato
Mario Ciampi, Florence/Florenz
Emilio Conti, Milan/Mailand
Cozzi e Scribani, Rome/Rom
Pino Dell'Aquila, Turin
Patrik Engquist, Stockholm
Dennis Gilbert, View, London
David Joseph, New York
Nick Kane, London
Sandro Lanciotti, San Benedetto del Tronto
Duccio Malagamba, Barcelona
Mihail Moldoveanu, Paris
Nacasa & Partners Inc., Tokio
Alfonso Perkaz, Navarra
Matteo Piazza, Milan/Mailand
Alberto Piovano, Milan/Mailand
Christian Richters, Münster
Phil Sayer, London
Pietro Savorelli, Florence/Florenz
Paul Warchol Inc., New York
Steve White, London
Irmfried Windbichler, Graz
Edward Woodman, London
Nigel Young, Foster and Partners, London
Miro Zagnoli, Milan/Mailand

Printed and bound
by Arti Grafiche Motta, Milan, Italy